Mom & Butch
Are
Dead Already

Mom & Butch
Are
Dead Already

POEMS

Sandra Bailey Browne

Surrogate Press®

Published in the United States by
Surrogate Press®
an imprint of Faceted Press®
Surrogate Press, LLC
Park City, Utah, USA
SurrogatePress.com

ISBN: 978-1-964245-20-1

This work is based

on

Unreliable Memories

And

Dreams

Dedicated

to

Mom & Butch

Table of Contents

Bedlam

In the snug, humid, bedroom
musty with Mom's Chantilly
Butch and I still shuttered off
for nap time, even at four and five.
The small room cramped
with Mom's slight bed
and two passed-down cribs
for Butch and me.

Sure, I could break out easily
from my rickety crib,
wake Mom, sleeping slouched
on the pantry table.
She would sigh as if I ached her heart,

shift her mouth all sad-mad
like the wax lips we melted
for fun on the heater.
It wasn't worth the cost,
disturbing Mom.
I remained still in my little prison,
in place.

But Butch was a spark.
He had no rules for stillness,
even used his club foot,
with the rocking chair brace.
Escaped by shoving his wrong foot
in a direction it had no plans to go.

He starred in a high-wire act.
Dreamed a crippled circus.
Vaulting over the side of his tiny jail
his crib's springs strained to squeal on him.
After he tired of the floor's freedom,
he would swing himself back,
dive into his soft, powdered prison
and fall easily into a deep sleep.

During my time in nap jail
my eyes forced a view
of heavy drapes hanging
from one dim window.

Odd, unfamiliar, reckless flowers,
dusty peach, yellow, and grays.
I studied their petals and stalks.
Without permission, the blooms turned
into mad monkeys, shadows on the ceiling
their strange jungle.

It was too much for my still baby-brain.
I worried that the truth may be so bendy.
Finally, with the jungle lurking too odd,
I worried into a nervous sleep.

Once, I smelled myself awake to
monkey forest smells, but it was Butch.
His little boy underwear by his side,
he was sorting his poop
like that king in his counting house.
Mom, drawn by the smell,
opened the door a crack,
peeked in to discover
her boy's messy offering.

I squinted my eyes to fake sleep.
She wasn't mad at my brother.
She picked him up and said so softly,
"Oh, my sweet Butchie Boy,
what the devil are you up to?"

And her sounds shook and confused me.
Not my Mom's quiet, soft words,
but the fright that the Devil
knew my brother's thoughts.

Rites

Blue laws groaned on in
1950's New England.
Only two spaces open
to Butch and me on Sundays:
Saint Mary's vampire church or
the dumpy Texaco station.

A thin, parched wafer
masquerading as Body at one,
Mom's nickel bribes, redeemed
into jawbreakers at the other.

My divorced Mom had a solid out
for missing Sunday Mass.
Vatican Bullies forbade her.

She traded her easy Sundays
for eternal damnation.
That was the deal.

Still, she offered us up, her two lambs.
Sent us off all scrubbed and wholesome.
Saint Mary's preached screwy sermons,
like limbo for babies unbaptized,
like hell for longing and lust,
like purgatory for minor, puny sins.

Still, fear and guilt snatched me up.
Marched me off to eight A.M. Mass
every eternal Sunday for five years.
From seven, as a true believer
at my first Communion,
to twelve, disenchanted
by Confirmation.
Where the priest spoke Latin
and we pew penitents didn't.

My wild brother, Butch
spirited off right at the start,
lost to this vague and judging god
along the mile ramble to Mass.
He discovered detours more bewitching, sparkling,
more sacred than the saving of
his perfect child's soul.

But I showed up, sat mute
in back pews until I didn't.
Bit by bit, I couldn't untangle
such confusing Canons.

The Son gathered
shiny-faced children
gently into His circle of care.
Loved us no matter what.

The Father scorned
my ordinary mother.
Then delivered her forever,
past all time ever created
to a sinister fiery hell.

Her Kind of Best

Mom coddled grievances,
ironed and folded them neatly
as if they were white linen.
Instead of dirty, dishwater wrongs
that were often technicolor legit.

Mom's arbiters formed a sulking line:
German tank, condemning, critic mother.
World-weary, work-weary, silent dad.
Casually neglectful, boozy older brothers.
Carnal, soulless boyfriends.
Exploitive, fake-liberal bosses.

This cramped antechamber bloated
with never-ending rancid demands
staged as a cacophony of rightful claims
inflicted with greedy velocity
while feigning goodwill.

Mom's muddled soul could at best,
prop a flimsy scaffolding in defense.
Mom was forever brain and body frazzled.
Worked ant hard. Twelve-and more-hour days.

Couldn't conjure up any fresh spells
for more than an anemic season.
Never shifted the house odds in her favor.
None held any light, any proper tender.

She reverted to mindless,
drab prickly options
when the brutal, plastic soldiers
set in their grimy snow globe attacked.
She weakly heaved swift
dissolving Kool-Aid anger.
Slugs of feeble words
lobbed at vague, gloomy
three-inch enemies,
but none hardly noticed.
They, too, had been rendered wrecked.

Mom would mix a contaminated cocktail:
a bottle or more of Ripple
with equal parts of useless pity
and empty righteousness.
She installed herself
in her maple rocking chair,
adjusting the faded,
purple printed cushion.
Sat in front of our small parlor window
with its cracked glass.

Staring out from our prized
second-story apartment.
A fine, four-season view,
if you gazed out with lifted chin,
cropping out our tenements'
six-car dirt driveway.

Mom in brief, bright seasons
could secret an irritant
into a tiny pearl of difference.
But could wield no iron to channel it
safely into her bleak heart-chamber.
Her voice of need
too mute, too alien
to propose minute compromises.
To insist on even flimsy, ragged armor.

Mom used up her thin,
precious, free time.
Allocated too many hours
ruminating on the long list
of rancid injustices,
like a starving rat
after the experiment is abandoned.

Her solutions spun no solutions at all.
Just weak words, hardly whimpers,
unheard by even herself,
mute, silent as ancient ooze.
No relevance to the imagined
fossilized creatures
that trampled powerfully
over her delusions, her dreams.

Mom's Small Country

You studied steep Willow Street.
Boasted grand oaks, maples, and pines.
Though only one willow.
Others had died.

In mild months, the scene offered
wooded splendor,
the fresh, budding green of the trees
the free wildflowers.
The first star of spring –
the forsythia bush.
Followed by dandelions,
Black-eyed Susans,
Later, poison sumac
Milkweed sheer joy with its
fluff dancing fluff.

I remember, particularly, Mom,
your delight and wonder
at the fragrant
purple wild lilacs.

You could savor
for whole afternoons
the fine perfume
that wafted generously
during the spring and summer.

But you drank too fast,
smoked too fast,
and even rocked too fast
in your maple rocker.

Mom, you could propel yourself
in that chair
inch-by-inch around the parlor,
drink in hand,
sloshing delicately
from your Tony-the-Tiger glass.

You seemed, for these moments,
to have your own cockeyed power.
Your own sad sovereignty.

Yet, still found yourself
at a familiar dead end;
even your bathroom threshold
proved too high by an inch
for your inadequate chariot.
You could calmly sit there.
In the rocker.

As if the un-view
of our small bathroom
with its peeled avocado linoleum
was just as pleasing and real
as the window's true view.
Perhaps you were dreaming.

If we kids needed the bathroom
we shoved you back away from the door,
slid by and used the toilet.
Maybe we got away
without washing our hands.

Or we might drag the rocker
with you, our woeful passenger
back to the true view.

Sometimes, we revolted.
Had enough of your moods,
we might decide to pretend-play violins.

You would shake your head.
Just add us kids to your pile of trials.

We loved you fiercely,
but your puzzled love confused us,
as much hot oil as soft baby powder.

We witnessed your honest grievances,
but we were too weak
to fix them or heal you.
So, we chose to laugh
without crinkling our eyes.
More of a mock.

Mom, you never spoke
in any true tongue,
to voice your tender, deep despair.

And without words to speak
you never could reach
your soul's remote province.

Good Times

The party is called to chaos.
Voices I know, others I don't.
I gawk at them from my bedroom.
Their sour smells invade, pushy.
Mom acts cheery, giddy.
In a too-sweet air,
she calls the drunks "Bunny",
same pet name she calls me.
When she's in a proper good mood.

It's after two, they file
into our tiny basement
after last call at Rocky's Bar,
the fixed point of this crowd's

measly planet.
Rowdy as swine,
their brassy bellowing
rubs me alert and stunned.

A big band forty-five starts exploding.
Mom is flirting,
giggling her boyfriend laugh.
Her over-ready fans
might turn away to discover her false teeth.
Worst, decaying black stubs before fixed
I could tell them facts like that.

A dumb lush fumbles,
enforcing the music volume.
His clumsy foot is hung up
on the brown cord
winding across Mom's
clean black and white floor.
The record player shutters
toward the edge.
It should fall. But it doesn't.

Romeo finally turns down
the band, spins,
grabs Mom's arm to dance.
She yanks herself away, huffy.

Her arm strikes the table.
She almost loses her high-heeled stride.

Records spew on the floor,
like shiny black baby flying saucers.
The boozy bunch hollows
a laugh too loud, too long.
No one rescues the records.

Mom's on to twinkling at another chump.
They dance. Too close.
Lots of noisy yakking. Yakking, yakking.
Smashed revelers
turn the music into screeds.

The forty-five is stuck, repeats, repeats.
No grownup hears it.
Butch finally has had enough.
Me too. Everything too much, too shrill.

He jumps up out of his bed next to me
scoots a couple steps into the kitchen,
flicks the record off the turntable
picks another one off the floor,
throws it on the turntable,
shoves the needle down.
It instigates a wobbly
Vaughn Monroe song.

Butch jumps back to bed.
The music groans;
it isn't an improvement.
It yanks at me, Butch too.
We are now sharp awake.

He deals me a glance; he has a plan.
A snoop mission.
We slide silently
out of our beds.

We poke around, moving like spooks.
We swig half-empty Buds.
Pick up change.
Even grab a couple of dollars,
from one lush's jacket.
Snuff out the Pall Malls
and foul stogies,
bothering us in Mom's
fancy-fake ashtrays.

The oil-stained, smelly mechanic grabs me.
Most nights, I swing fast,
avoid being cornered.
But tonight, when the sleaze
catches me,
I'm snagged and can't seem
to bother Mom.

He sways and stoops over,
leers me eye level.
Tries to kiss me;
geez, I'm nine for God's sake.
I bite his lip, bloody;
he shoves me hard away.
Butch catches my eye,
we grin at my win.

The face of the red and white cat
with the ticking tail says four.
Booze squeezes time for the fools.
Not for us kids.
Minutes and hours spread thick.
The bash keeps moving
a jerking black-and-white movie.

The mean shindig fades
as dawn butts in.
Fake friendships go sober.
Dull strangers once again.

And we kids, tired
and bad-tempered,
get ready for school.
Tiptoe around Mom
as she cleans up the sour mess.
Chaste and silent.

Butch's Report

The sign at the entry announces,
"Home for Little Wanderers."
It's apropos.
The boys regularly run away
from their nagging injustices.

The boys who count
no visitors Sunday
nor a stream of Sundays past give up.
Their bewildered thoughts
unravel them.
They mostly blame themselves.
They wouldn't visit their own selves.

Last week, John and Ben
ran off together on Monday,
charged with emptying
the garbage after supper out back.
Each boy struggled to hold a side handle
of the heavy, dirty garbage can.
Near as tall as the boys' eight-year-old selves.

They peered into the dining room window,
checked if the indifferent staff had
beady eyes on them.

Then both, just dropped the can.
Without really conspiring,
started hightailing
down the long alley
to Route 6.

Here's the kicker;
instead of escaping
they sprinted along together.
(John even reached out
and grabbed Ben's hand
for some reason.)

And the two just ran in circles
around their prison.
Past the escape route.
Their feet remembered
they had nowhere, really, to go.

Cost of Getting By

Hours stretched slower,
longer in winter.
Mom walked two miles into dawn
to her eight-hour shift
at the woolen mill by Cargill Falls.

Mom and the other women
in too hot, humid summers
in heatless, frigid winters
pulled the heavy woolen bolts
yard by yard, across their laps,
sought out the tiny defects,
meticulously mended
the small-sized holes to invisible
in the fine, rich worsted.

Then, after eight hours,
without a moment's rest
mom willed herself
another longer, slower mile uphill
to homes with kept lawns,
flower gardens, columns.
Housekeeper-cook-nanny
for the mill owners' families.

Mom left her second shift
often after dark,
bone weary, worn out
in a work-anesthetizing trance.
She walked the last mile home.
No streetlights.
She clocked her steps.
Her feet programmed to our home.
The stars and moon she missed.

Mom's decent bosses might half-ask
to drive her home; they had two cars.
She would say something stupid.
"Oh, the walk will do me good."
The worst and even the best
of the exchequers
would pretend to believe her.

They also believed in you, Mom,
when they whispered indiscretions
to their convenient confessor.
Then, only when it was all too much,
did you puncture their secrets.

Mom, you chose me, too often, to tell.
The exposing served as gaudy,
meager, hot-air revenge.
I was powerless, a feeble Oracle.
An unformed, well-trained monkey
clinging to your barbed wire body.

I studied fast, each coiled crime,
snared in powerless Greek tragedies.
I offered worthless,
soothing salves, unctuous balms.
I mutated into a silent Cassandra,
with a severed tongue.
Caught in an exhausting,
numbing loop.
Nodding my head.
Agreeing with Mom's truth.
Yes. "Yes, Mom."

Mom's Wiles

Mom hid behind doors to pounce out
with her banshee scream.
We mostly liked being scared.
But our night times could turn on us.

She told us real, ugly landlord stories.
He might be standing over us when we slept.
Since he really did have a key to get in.
But Mom said he smelled so bad,
no way he could go undetected.

She pretend stabbed her hand
with the can opener,
using seafood sauce blood
and raw hamburger clots.

Once she poked her wrist for real
opening a can of corn.
Now, that was real blood!
But she was brave as a bear,
maybe for our sake.

Grabbed a rag and just
moved on to some distraction
"Hey, look at that thing,"
diverting us to the window.
But our eyes were stuck on the blood
seeping through the soaked rag.

She rechristened food:
     spaghetti - albino worms
     melted butter - bird blood
     sauerkraut - skunk inners

Sometimes, Mom used up
her sparse off-work time
just for us.
She cut Putnam Patriot
into train shapes.
Transformed into engines, box cars, cabooses.

Enough that they ran circling
the entire perimeter of our tiny kitchen.

Or folding shiny Time pages
into a whole squadron of planes.
Teaching us how to make more
than the basic kid plane.

We took turns flying them out
our second-story window.
The winner got the same as the loser
Chocolate Junket.
We loved Junket!

Luring us on night walks
to check out who and what
was out and about.
Mom's flashlight could be fake defective.

Blinking on and off.
She tucked in creepy growls
to scare what might scare us.

Showing us, on too-long walks,
how to pee squatting
on the side of the road.
Though even country roads might surprise
with sudden car lights.
So, we were fast at peeing.

Mom might tip us over
if she finished her pee first.

On Easter Eve, Mom took the time
to situate jellybeans on all the chair rails.
Maybe two hundred of them.
She didn't ever set the same
two colors as neighbors.
That was something.

Mom let us use knives
that could poke our eyes out.
Though she only gave us soft things,
bananas and cooked beets to decapitate.
She hid them after Butch
chased the babysitter for no reason
with one of the big butcher knives.
He spoiled it for both of us.

Mom could be coaxed
into yanking out her false teeth.
Boy, did we like that one.
Rolling her eyes up in her head
so only the whites showed.

Mom and us kids,
in those finest moments,
alone, no outside snoopers
in a timeless, charmed sandbox.

Boredom

Bored as slugs.
No place to go, nothing to do.
But Butch and I would get moving fast
when Mom said, all fussy, "Oh, I can fix that.
I've got rat stuff to clean."
Absolutely sure there was no stuff of the rat
we were interested in cleaning.

We would find the dirty, pink rubber ball
abandoned in the dandelion weeds.

Throw it up against Mrs. Lester's
six-foot fieldstone wall, all craggy,
crafted the game even more tricky.
One: fling it under our leg,
Two: toss it and turn around fast to catch
Three: pitch it clapping quickly three times.
We could play forever, well, in kids' time,
until one of us wore dull at losing.

We might shift to the dogwood bush
and pick and squish the Japanese beetles.
Later, when the day grew into dusk,
retrieve our mason jars with the nail holes
and collect fireflies.

We could only keep them for ten minutes.
Mom said they didn't appreciate being in jar jail.
Would we? No, but we wouldn't want
to be squished like beetles either.
But the shiny bugs really
could gnaw oodles of leaves.
Mom said we would have left them alone
if they had been reasonable.

When it grew fully dark,
we switched to yanking nightcrawlers.
Sold a penny-a-piece to Mr. Zeller.
Even though he never fished.

Mom said he fried them and ate them,
but that was a joke.

Mom would let Butch use a butter knife
"So, you don't kill somebody"
to carve green-brown spears
out of the forsythia branches.
Mom painted a bullseye on a towel rag
and nailed it up on our colossal maple,
all gnarly ghost roots.

In early spring, the spears were too floppy to
pierce the towel. So, I had the idea to use stones.
I struck Butch once while he was
holding up the sagging target.
He howled but clammed up
when Mom ran outdoors.
I claimed it as an accident. He just shrugged.
But still, he could get on my last nerve.

We played hopscotch by the decrepit garages.
I found lovely flat stones to pitch.
Butch picked fat, more round stones.
Usually, I won.
Though, once he wised up,
choosing better stones,
he may have won more games than I did.
But my memory won't fess up to that.

One whole summer, maybe my favorite ever,
Butch and I spent hours every day cracking rocks
open with bigger rocks to find silver.
We stored old pillowcases full of split rocks
in the back basement.

Turns out it was mica.
Some know-it-all grownup had the specifics.
As if we cared.

The Too Permanent Permanent

Mom posed at the screen door
in her checked pedal pushers,
smoking her Pall Malls,
"Sandi, I have spare time.
Come on in, and we can doll you up.
You're going to love it!"
I thought, darn, there goes my Sunday.

So, what if I was just sitting on the steps.
Staring out at our dirt yard.
Couldn't she figure that for kids,

that was plenty to do.
I was not. Really not. Going to love it.

She would just throw an old sheet
down on the kitchen floor,
plunk me on the pine stool, her infliction site.
The three-hour treatment:
tiny pink curlers,
a few hair strands from prior inflictees,
the pee-acid stink.
Mom's cigarette smoke.

I, resigned and gloomy,
handed Mom one
thin white paper at-a-time.
At the end of the torment,
Stupid-magic-tight-as-girdle curls

"You love your new look?"
She seemed to have a short recall.
The waves consistently tight, kinky.
Not one time did they prettify me.

I sensed such hare-brained favors
reduced the storms that brewed in her head,
in no way connected to the hair on mine.

Mom subjected me too often to
Toni's New and Improved Wave.
The $3.00 layout swore to fix straight hair,
the results promised brighter
and bouncy and soft waves.
Oh, but didn't stop at the roots.
Life itself would be monumentally changed.

Its promises were as fake as
Mom's falsies betraying her
while diving into slimy, dead fish
Lake Quinebaug on Memorial Day.
Her rubber bosoms bobbing
about the surface.

Mom's act was equally misguided
as she fiddled with my brown, straight locks.
I smelled whiffs of burning hair,
fried to coal split ends.
Same smell as when Mom saddled up
too close, lighting the Kerosene burner.
The first cold snap of fall.
Mom's singed, crinkly eyebrow worms,
evidence the season had shifted.

Sure, I ached for Mom's meager ministrations, but
I rated our time with Toni as a tedious sacrifice.
Jesus, straight hair didn't seem tragic to me.

Yet, as much as I saw no compelling reason
to get a permanent ever,
quite a few of Mom's mill friends
signed up as volunteers for that same ordeal.
They supposed they liked the results.

Yet, Mom offered more to her fans
than the sham of shiny, Clairol waves.
A few beers, some sour cream, and herring,
silky forty-five's; Ink Spots,
Frankie Lane, Jo Stafford, Peggy Lee.
She was funny, too, offered plenty of hoots,
often at the neighbor's expense.

These tough gals plain relished
Mom's good-humored gossip,
her conspiratory company.
A break in their dull days.
And what the hell, hair grows back.

Amends

Claire, dear friend,
I distanced myself from you
as if poverty were contagious.
I inflicted a daily prayer of
unkind, silent judgments
on your wrinkled and sour dresses,
that could have been washed and ironed
like Mom did my dresses,
even working two jobs.

Yet, I ignored the mom I knew you to have.
Saddled with five Catholic brats
she could barely move her slight,
statue self, sitting collapsed for hours
at the second-story tenement window.
Stunned and deaf to the
unrelenting howls your tribe made.

How could she take it?
How could you?

You played with your torn paper dolls,
missing limbs and tabs,
right in the middle of the kitchen floor.
Outfits you cut from brown paper bags.
Colored with your older sister's discarded
lipsticks and eye shadows.

Sweaty flesh and your anemic bloodlines
jumping and shoving into and over you.
You hunched, entranced over your paper kids
on the cracked linoleum floor
your mom covered with newspaper.
It kept it fresh, she thought or wished.
She had scrambled egg ideas.

But how could anybody think in the din?
Always background laments,
kids bawling, screeching finally,
down to tired whimpers at dusk.
You should have had real meals
with vegetables like my mom fixed
instead of cornflakes
for almost every summer supper.
Switched to soup in winter.
Cabbage was that season's stench.

I knew all about your life.
I was sitting downstairs alone.
Butch in some other jail.
I listened in the nervous quiet
till Mom came home later than usual.
Well, later than I longed for.

Scarcity bred so much chaos in our families.
All kinds of late bills,
grownups scrambling always,
to delay dollars to the gas and electric guys.
Mr. Anderson, our worm of a landlord
exacted our weekly rent of $15.
It would be a bit overdue,
and then a bit more.
He hissed at Mom till Mom somehow
discharged the debt.

Claire, rich people smell better than poor people.
You knew that.
Except for my family, we were raw clean,
but then Mom was cleaning more than dirt.
None of your sisters and brothers
passed my daily military inspection
oily hair, dirty nails, sores that stayed.

Poor people played their music louder, too.
Their radios served up more static than songs.
Did it drown out the drum
of our families' shame?
Our too-old, bone-weary mothers,
angry, impotent fathers, when we had one.
You did. I didn't.

Claire, I didn't want to be near poor kids
after a while, worrying on Wednesday.
Threats of no milk till Friday's payday.
I had nightmares of cereal in cupboards
too high for you to reach.

So, I released the futile efforts
of trying to raise all sinking ships.
You, Claire, were one of the sinking ships.
I got tired of scouring your green teeth
with baking soda and bleach.
You were patient but weary, too.

Even then, I brought another ship home,
Edie, to wash her hair,
rid her lice, squash them all.
Instead, I caught them; they were hardy.
All my misguided child efforts
were a pathetic, exhausting game.

Feeble Intentions

Tippy, our mutt, our protector for 15 years,
jumped up and bit through Johnny's pants
when he swung at Mom drunk.
My sweet furry soldier would have more years
if we hadn't waited so long to save
the seven dollars for the cheap vet
we never saw before or after.

By then, my ten-pound Tippy
had grown a two-pound tumor.
By then, all that was left was her dying.

I took her to a winter party.
I couldn't say no to the invitation

that hinted at more.
She was in a shoe box swathed
in a scrap of blue wool from the mill.
I took her down to the basement
by the furnace, rumbling warmth
By then, she wouldn't eat.
She could take an eyedrop of water every hour.

On the third trip down the stairs, she was still.
I sobbed and bawled, curled over her body.
Feeling familiar shame and stabbing remorse.
My new boyfriend and his friends came down.
Lined up on the stairs.

And formed a silent chorus.

Liberty

In summer 1954 most people in my hometown
never even traveled
to Providence, Rhode Island,
just thirty miles away.

So, it was a big deal when Mom and me,
Aunt Ronnie, my mom's only sister
and her son, my cousin Peter
went to New York City.

Peter was thirteen. I was eleven.
Butch couldn't come.

He was at Meriden School for Boys.
Mom said he was having his own adventure.

We were all so ecstatic!
We donned Sunday clothes.
Mom bought me a pair of white Mary Janes.
Peter had a clip-on tie, in red.
All of us gals even wore white gloves.

We had tickets on this fancy train.
Plush seats and a dressed-up conductor
it took us about two and a half hours
to get there. It seemed shorter,
we were having fun.

Peter and I got to sit separately
from our mothers.
We bounced all over the train car.
Switching from side to side,
seeking the best view.
Or just because we could.

And our moms let us be.
No "behave your wild boar selves,"
one of mom's favorite fusses.
They just noticed each other.

That was a treat I guess, just sister talk.
Work, kids and men often butt in on that.

Once we arrived in New York,
we were dumped into Penn Station.
It was massive and loud
with odd train announcements.
Rushing men, dolled up-women,
Startled children and babies.
All manner of outfits.
Some left odd smells as they passed,
not bad, just new and different.

We walked a short way
in single file to the hotel.
That was quite a carnival in itself.
The colorful crowd
colliding in opposite directions.
We came to the Dixie in Times Square.
Mom checked us in at the desk.
She was lovely and calm.
There was no glitch in getting the key.

We climbed the stairs to our room.
Aunt Ronnie nixed the elevator.
She was always on the timid side.
It was pretty small. Looked a little rickety too.

We reached our room on the third floor.
The small space had two beds and a dresser,
left hardly any room for us.

The wallpaper was faded green.
The toilet was rusty.
I had no judgment at the time.
Just excited that we were in New York.

Years later Johnny Carson
made snide jokes about this very hotel.
I felt a tinge of shame.
That by then was a habit of mine.

That first evening in New York,
I remember like a movie I saw yesterday.
Uncle Danny came to our room after work.
He brought some fish and chips in newspaper
and ice-cold Moxie.

We spread it all out on our beds.
And knelt to eat it. Kind of a tasty communion.
The window was wide open.
We could hear the din of the city.
It was raucous and exciting.
We laughed louder and smiled wider
We were all so happy, I knew it to be true.

Uncle Danny was dressed
in a fine gray suit and tie.
Mom worked in the woolen mills
so we knew our wools.
A suit to go to work?
Plain impressive.

He worked right in New York City.
He took a train at night
home to Long Island.
He read the paper and just relaxed.
Could even take his shoes off on the train.

Uncle Danny was married to my Aunt Dena,
at the time they had one son Chris.
Owned their home,
bought it with the GI Bill.
He could have been shot to death
for that benefit.
But he wasn't, Granny said her prayers
brought him back alive.

Uncle John, Uncle George, Uncle Tommy
all came back too from the war.
Uncle Bobby didn't go,
had some problem that kept him out.
So he stayed and worked in the mills.
He was my second favorite uncle.

Our family considered
of all our relatives
Uncle Danny had made it.
The Army work got him that great job.
Though I can't say I knew what he did.

Uncle Danny's wife, Aunt Dena
wasn't Mom's flavor.
They rarely visited us.
Although by then they had a
new secondhand station wagon.
Mom knew it was Dena's doing.
But really, I could make a long list
of why-nots to visit our clan.
Won't go into that.

Dena was short and Italian dark,
wore fancy clothes
so she wasn't obligated to do anything
during their rare visits.
Couldn't even set the table for god's sake.

She sat and smoked Camels
with her elbow on her waist
and her wrist turned up.
Mom said, "Who does she think she is?"
It wasn't a real question.

Aunt Dena would die in a few years of lung cancer,
just six months after delivering David.
Uncle Danny never married again.

I had a hard time sorting that all out.
Mom said, "Well Dena's in heaven".
I don't think she even believed it.
In heaven that is. Her tone said
Let's move off that subject.

Our priests mentioned heaven
but sitting in the pews on Sunday
we spent a whole lot more time
in Purgatory. Like hundreds of years!
What was the point?

Of course, we didn't know Dena's fate
right then on that grand evening
in exotic, singular New York.
So, we enjoyed Uncle Danny's company
without grief and guilt.

He was kind and asked us kids easy questions.
"Is your teacher doing right by you?"
He was funny and generous.
He gave a five-dollar bill to Peter and me.
"Can you take these fives off of me?
That's my unlucky number."

After we finished eating
we walked around and saw all the lights.
The new cars, all black and shiny.
The bright theatres on Broadway.
One announcing the Pajama Game.
All those grandly dressed going to the musical.

Uncle Danny held my hand.
He wished he didn't have to work
so he could be our tour guide.
All us four hugged him when he left.
I wished often we had more men like him
back in our hometown.

We were in grand New York for
three more days. It went by too-too fast.
Over the speed limit
for my memories to keep up.

No museums, I remember,
but we saw a true flea circus, in an alley.
Peter and I were impressed.
Butch would have been too.

Also saw Albert/Alberta
half-woman, half-man.
I felt a little sad for that person.
But he/she was a good sport.

Mom was more comfortable
with all that than Aunt Ronnie.

Mom bought a Sunday New York Times
for Butch, he would have appreciated that.
He had a lot of time for reading
loved to read about different ways of living
while he waited for his life to get going.

We ate at the famous Port Arthur.
It was a swanky Chinese place.
Glittering fabrics and lanterns, deep carpets.
Chinese waiters rushed quietly.
Music new though tuneless to my ears.
The artistry of the menu was lovely,
the food too exotic for my taste.
But the newness and glamour
was so festive, I filled up on that.

Another precious blue-sky day
we boarded a ferry
chugged through rough water
out to the Statue of Liberty.

I didn't know how to swim.
I was worried and uneasy.
The tenders hung grimy and old.
Also, I worried a little seasick,
a threat in the back of my throat.

An old woman with a kerchief did throw-up
The crew was somehow so cheerful
about cleaning up the mess.

Once we arrived, we took a full tour
and learned the statue's index finger
was eight feet long.
She had been a 350-piece gift from France.
Sailing all the way across the ocean.
Who thinks up gifts like that?
Well, the French.

My Grandpa had come over
from Lithuania at twelve
with his mom and sister Mae.
So Ellis Island was a special place for us
It welcomed people like my grandpa.

I have a cherished faded photo
of us four in Times Square,
none of us look exactly happy.
We may have felt out of our league.
I did feel that, but too,
a sense of amazement and awe.
And a seed of knowing and promise...

Blown Away

In 1955 my town's own Quinebaug River
overflowed like an angry whale misplaced.
Eighty-seven deaths were reported
throughout New England.

For my dumb child self
the worst part of the angry storms?
The previously well-behaved magnesium stacked
in a plant on the river exploded.
That's what chemistry dictated it did
when mixed with water.

Grown-ups took their time to explain
what was happening.
It was during the Cold War.

My best surmise
after all those air-raids practices?
The Russians were invading.

Mom and I were waiting it out
over at Aunt Ronnie's place.
Relatives and friends,
coming and going.
Maybe moving felt safer to them.

The grownups ferreted out fresh news
on a scratchy blue portable radio.
There was warm beer
drunk by loud men.
I swigged a bit of left-overs
it tasted sour, so no solution.

I was cold, cold, fear shredded me
though it was steamy summer.
Butch was away
in Meriden at that time.
Mom couldn't get through
to him on our party line
till the third day.
And what felt like her hundredth try.

The chaos stayed wild for days.
I kept shivering, and whining
Hail Marys and Our Fathers
to keep me alive.
Mom and Butch too.
I was young.

The grownups moved around me
like I was a chair
I, the only one who saw me.
The rains and winds and explosions
went on for such a long-long time
in my child mind.

I became weary, gave up on my stale prayers.
They collected in a sieve,
draining faster than my creed
could replace them.

I sat silent and numb
and shifted my theology
  there is no Jesus,
  there is no Mary
there would be no one to save me.
Yet I did survive.

After it was over, I felt out of tune.
Those who did not lose their home
or their child or pet seemed to be almost giddy
with their "Thank God!" "Prayers to our Father!"

I thought, "Now wait a minute!
What about the 87 people who died?"
And it pierced my soul
with an ugly fractured fact.
Even good moms and dads and kids lost homes,
lost pets and some their too new lives.

I felt an awkward gratitude for my family's survival
as if our three spaces would be better filled
by more worthy candidates.
But my mind tossed out that too evolved idea.
I wilted confused and muddled.
My life just might be
the luck of the draw.

Putnam's population in 1950 was 9304, in 1960 it was 8412.
In 2020 it was 9354, 50 people more than in 1950!

Faith Derailed

Two years after our grand visit to New York,
Aunt Ronnie, at 38, gave birth
to a precious baby boy, Michael.
Three months later she was dead.

From childhood, she suffered from a rheumatic heart
and the pregnancy and delivery
proved lethal a few months later.

After Aunt Ronnie's death,
while our family still mourned,
our precious baby was taken away
and sent to Eddie's mother
a dozen miles away in Killingly.

My cousin Peter went to live
with Grandpa and the "boys,"
our two grown uncles who never married.
It was as if a flamingo had to board with three boars
No ill intentions but still a clumsy fit.

No one in our family
ever saw the baby again.
He ended up living with Eddie
and his dumpy new wife.

Peter continued to be angry
with his mother for dying.
Blame eases pain. Perhaps.
Though he fared much
better after high school.
He headed to New York City,
found a position at Samuel A. French
publishing. And stayed till he retired.
It became a true home.

Grannie had died the year before at
56 of a heart attack.
She was built like a thick brick
and we all thought without thinking
that she would live forever.
She had steered the family hull.

Grandpa was sweet and weak
and the boys ran all over him.

The women, all gone now too,
except for mom.

Mom After Time

Violent tableaus, dark colors.
I heard your breath, fast and aching.
Or not at all, held in terror.
My psyche stored more
than reason could remember.

Truths calcified in caves.
Much later, swooping down unguarded
times. These memories swift and too close,
returned like rabid bats.

While still haunting me,
I willed daring to free the traps.
Memories escaped freshly, as raw regards.
After all, she is dead, and I am alive.

An unconscious search
ruled in the background.
Fueled by my deep aching, missing.
Like a cure, unveiled a litany of
graces from her. Glinted in the dark
and narrow caves of my losses.
I, without intention, strung a new rosary.

I perceived more clear-eyed, kindlier,
so settled and worn into my own long life,
I absolved Mom's willing blindness,
dreary neediness, sad betrayals.

This frail, imperfect mother
that is now reflected in myself,
can now look back, look up,
with awe and wonder at my own mothering.

A gentle, loving resignation toward her,
toward this singular creature I was assigned to.
She crafted so much right,
having been bequeathed so little mothering.

Class Action in California

The Morgans' never-used
pristine pool was ignored
except when they escaped, chauffeured away
down the circle drive for a grand cruise.
Mom thought up fast,
who could borrow,
benefit from such luxury.

She gave her collaborators the clear.
Her clan, buddies, peripheral pals,
almost before the driveway was cool.
They descended like an alliance
of weird lemurs high on millipedes.

Mom could fashion
an impressive poolside soirée.

Without exact consent,
the Morgans' bestowed swanky booze,
grand hotel white towels,
and close-to-the-cost-of-a-car outdoor grill
serving up top-grade steaks.

Even the air was pristine.
Forty-two rich aroma rosebushes.
Borders of sweet Jasmine.
High-class, fragrant smells.

Overtime Mom staged a half-dozen
of these Cinderella socials
for her ragamuffin waifs.
For a night, they believed wholly
in the rightness
to receive such largeness.

The gift of such nights held memories
that were vivid and immediate.
Could be resurrected
scene after scene by Mom
and her confederates year after year.
In the winter, over a beer.
In the summer, at a picnic.
Their grand yarns would be resuscitated.

The reciting was a method of feeling
as good, as whole, as privileged,
as they believed themselves to be
on the true night itself.
Their almost sacred retellings
became dream prayers.
Fables of a kind.
Mom luxuriated in being the agent of goodness
even if rooted in such transgressions.

Mrs. Morgan tried only once
to pin Mom down
in their seventeen seasons together.
Those Midwestern zealots snitched on Mom,
"Oh, the commotion was so unruly it was,
well, plain devilish."

True, the police had been called that one time.
When the blue goons arrived that night,
They were just lovely to Mom.
"Keep it down, and you'll be fine."
Nothing more was thought of it.

Then, weeks later, Mrs. Morgan
brought the illicit soiree up to Mom
Mom's defense, when Mrs. Morgan
timidly accused her?

Mom searched the ceiling, put her hands out,
palms up, like she was being offered Communion,
or imploring a part-time angel.

"I will not defend myself
for having a little companionship
as I suffer your absence,
as I looked after your precious property."

Mom began gaining traction,
continued believing herself
righteous and innocent
of the crime of trespassing on their land.
Bereft of society
into a kaleidoscope
of rare conviviality and elegance
for that singular night.
Really, hardly a mortal, or even venal sin.

Mom felt righteously offended
started for the pantry exit,
still pumping out words of justification,
collected her sweater and purse,
steamed toward the back door.

Mrs. Morgan wrinkled her linen handkerchief
dabbing her nose and patting her chest
broke rank with the neighbors.

"Well, now Maggie, let's just calm down,
just forget about it,
Midwesterners are so starchy."

Mrs. Morgan took her sizable bulk,
turning about face, she propelled herself
with her girlish, tiny steps
soundlessly back to her bedroom suite.
She closed the door as she murmured
Strict regrets to herself
to never, ever mention
such minor transgressions again.

*Mom's Last Best Job, age 62 to 81, was for the Morgans.
Their cruises continued, as did mom-sponsored carnivals.
Years later, Mom received seventeen thousand dollars
from the Morgan Estate. One thousand dollars for each
year of service. Mom seemed embarrassed.*

Sacrament

The last time I visited my brother,
two days before his birthday.
Dreary June, 1999.
He had been collected off the streets,
again unconscious, by the cops.
Delivered to a second-rate nursing home.
He was a regular at one or another
of the low-slung buildings with dirt for grass
hunched along the poor-rent stretch of Fair Oaks.

The outfit wasn't much,
a common cocktail; piss and bleach.
Safer than the city alleys.
Offered a proper bed,
fed food, he called 'school cafeteria slop.'

The proforma nurse titled him my "father".
He was that physically ravaged.
He had shrunk, always smaller,
thinner than the last time,
sunburned to a varnished mummy.

As Mom and I reached his bedside,
a facility's doctor there,
Mom fluttered her hand at me,
entreating me, 'talk to him.'
I moved quietly to this god's side and bowed.
As if being obsequious
could affect my brother's outcome.
I babbled about "Going forward".

Silence, more silence,
He sighed in six syllables,
"He's not "going forward.
He used up all his prayers."

I fidgeted, shamed by my bloated hope.
Butch and Mom continued
feigning fascination
at the TV's Spanish game show.
The doctor patted his shoulder.

Left the scene.
Mom and Butch came to,
shifted their fake attention
from the TV to me.

Mom swallowed hard a few times.
Decided it was a perfect time
to visit the other sons
of other mothers.
His Road Dog is what Butch called Mom.
Yet, guilt reduced her comfort cards.
She was numb after years of visits to
her maimed son's ruinous remains.

Instead, she brought cigarettes and candy
for him and other patients.
"Friends," she called them.
In truth, just other men
dying too soon.

After Mom wandered off
silence bore down too long.
Butch risked a glance at me.
Mouthed quietly, perhaps exhaling sins.
"I'm going to hell."
Some seconds passed. Infinity.

I reached over and softly brushed his forehead.
Daring the kindness of a kiss.

    he was the baby
    the toddler
    the child
    the teen
    the man
all rushing into this scared
and sacred moment.

I took his hand, cradled it.
It was trembling, cold.
I mumbled, without pretense
"I believe God has already forgiven you."
(It could be true.)
He unstiffened.

Forty hours later
his lifetime of bewildered being was over.

Ember

During the three days
you assigned for dying, Mom,
I mourned and resurrected
a dark bloom of arcane
and unwelcomed despair.
Drummed in me the blighted
initiations of your birth:
the brutal granite poverty,
the casual indifference,
the stale severity
of your family's particular
suffocating province.

Into that household,
you, Magdalene Theresa,
in 1921, labored into.
It forced a harsh, cloistered order.

The inheritance,
to its females;
an infected gut of shame
and longing
stuck as if forever in dreary
New England Februarys.

Five hard, tough brothers,
one sickly rheumatic sister,
and you, the default Cinderella,
endlessly botched the prince part.
Your mother, Eva Gaus,
carved up and served you
helpings and helpings
of disappointed hostility.

You smuggled her legacy of disappointments
like blind snakes
naked and hidden, inside you
and struck at those you loved— could not
stomach their ridiculous dreams.

Yet, you were graced
with a few gentle female angels
assigned to counter-mother you.

You hammered together a rickety bridge.
Peered past, to witness anew
the missed opportunities.
You, dear mother,
had been too poor, soul-sick,
ignorant, bereaved, to dream.

The daring of your death's finality
near cornered, treed me, your daughter
into some modest tin mettle.

As I sat a borrowed shiva,
"Mom, what do you wish
you could have been?"

You raised your head,
crowned by striking white hair,
a slightly frumpy halo.
You looked with
direct astonishment into my eyes.
Your eyes bore bright.

Your arms, slumped by your side
in your wheelchair, lifted, swept, gracefully,
palms out, bestowing to me,
a true and deep oblation.
Perhaps body and blood.

"Oh! Why yes,"
as if you were awaiting
that vital inquiry your 88 years.
And in delight, you sang
"Why, a dancer, of course!"

My Directive

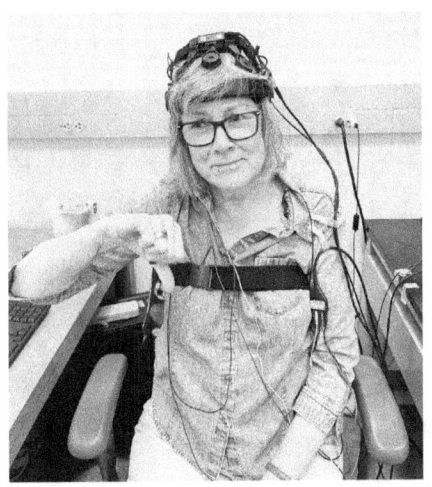

I hope to choose my dying season.
Late spring would be best.
Both Mom and Butch checked out
the same month they tumbled into the world.
So, June would be perfect for me.

I want to die at home
get a good night's rest
before I head out.
Not the impossible bright light,
noisy hallways, too clean smells
where I can be awakened,
for inconsequential measurement.

I'm eighty for God's sake
If I'm in the hospital,
no extra falderal.
The only observation
I want the nurse to note:
"She is dry and toasty."

I'll likely exit the hospital
"against doctor's orders."
I'll call an Uber and flee home,
grateful for un-antiseptic air.
I'll retrieve the key, open the door
take a quick nap.
I want to luxuriate in my cozy home.
I want death, that will be novel enough,
to happen in this sweet familiarity.
With my beloved fur child,
Sadie, by my side,
being sweetly and reliably indifferent.

My extravagant yearning, just a few friends
funny and kind dropping by with their
uniquely talented gifts:
        Rossie reciting her bawdy poems
        Mataji dancing around my happy sick bed
        Gayle bouncing in with a 4-star soup.
        Norma with her guidelines for kindness

Joanne, her highly efficient on-target self.
Sarah with her sonorous voice
reading a few juicy pages of Ulysses

And then there are soul provisions:
   rhubarb pie
   fried clams
   green tea ice cream
   pork chops and sauerkraut
   Chocolate Junket
   Franco American spaghetti
   malt balls
   Mackintosh apples

Other wishes: wash my hair every two days.
My scalp is tender, so watch it.
Post daily shower, slather my rickety body
with Jergens Original.
Dress me in my Petit Plum pajamas.
Cremate me in them too.
Clean crisp, white sheets changed daily.
Windows opened to light, to air,
to the music of everyday.

I might choose to
shove off the shelves
all dusty highbrow tomes.

Rewatch Judge Judy,
and True Crime.

Listen to Jerry Lee Lewis,
James Brown, Edith Piaf,
Willie Nelson. Etta James.
I call foul to "Suffering is ennobling."
I will arrange a larcenous friend to
slip me some illicit pills
When I assess my pain
is slight or agony — my call.

My family can meander over
For brief visits
I'm gently resigned
I don't need much from them now.
Tell me about fun stuff
from their normal, fully alive lives.
We can laugh together.
After a few minutes
I can toss them free
rerouting them back into the thicket
of their astonishing days.

In these, my final hours
I heave away my wrongs.
I have overdone the apologies and regrets.

No breast-beating.
Turn the dial to a little empathy
for myself and those I loved
and tried to.
Appreciate a few soft lies
and honest truths
during my dying season.
Choose to shrug aside it all.
I sense the divine.
I feel peaceful, transcendent,
even roguishly angelic.

Finally

I still come from kerosene stoves
and cracked magnolia floors.
From easy shotguns and rusting animal traps.
I come from rickety porch steps
and dirt where lawns used to be.
From empty sour Bud bottles
and free but costly government cheese.
I come from Grandpa's garden
with real tomatoes and corn.
My uncles' fresh caught trout.
From Black-eyed Susans and
pine needle beds.
I come from fat rats and moldy basements.
From police sirens and used-up pick-ups.
I come from chipped nails
and abscessed teeth.
From flat stares and fake promises.
I come from white cotton blouses
and Catholic uniforms.
Deep genuflects and unholy water.
I come from a dog-tired mother
and abused then absent brother
and seven-dollar support checks.
From revolving babysitters

and uninvited social workers.
I come from dismissive nods
and hostile head turns.
From zirconium rings
and adult silent, furtive sex.
I come from sweet, dazzling libraries
and magic carpet books.
From transvestite angels and gurus
and gentle guides.
I come from nightmares and reruns.
Though, finally, unlikely sacraments
and reckless redemptions.

Dedication and Acknowledgement

This book is consecrated to Sadie Bear Flufferton, Lolly Pop, and Tootsie Roll, my three Chow Chows who lay sleeping beside me as I wrote over the last thirty-two years. Their snoring, my metronome.

All three had the same lovely habit during their reign. They would punctuate their deep sleep by an alarm unheard by me, stand up and pad nearer, nose to knee, and give me a solemn look that I think meant "You got it." But could have meant "You're bored." It didn't matter, because sometimes while writing I did have it and other times well, I was bored. My fur muses would then turn away and plop back into slumber.
Message sent. Message received.

Importantly each member of the trinity, because of the unwavering sweetness of their animal nature, stood in for all my cherished teachers, colleagues, friends, family— alive and passed—who were and are in their gentle way kind and encouraging to my creative efforts.

And so,
I persist…

Biography

Sandra Bailey Browne has been writing poetry for a few dozen years about her childhood and other confusing subjects. She has practiced her craft in two writing groups that have met throughout these years. She has attended several of the University of Iowa's summer writing workshops.

Sandra was the first in her extended family to attend college, receiving a BA and MA in Human Development. Her life's work was in child welfare which included directing an international adoption agency, local homeless shelters, and country family services. Sandra has spent her retirement writing with moments of sky diving, receivingan anime tattoo, and taking ukulele lessons.